Inspirations

for the

Awakening Soul

Inspirations

— *for the* —

Awakening Soul

Rhonda S. McBride, Ph.D, LCDC

BALBOA.
PRESS

A DIVISION OF HAY HOUSE

Balboa Press books may be ordered through booksellers or by contacting:

Balboa Press
A Division of Hay House
1663 Liberty Drive
Bloomington, IN 47403
www.balboapress.com
1-(877) 407-4847

Because of the dynamic nature of the Internet, any web addresses or
links contained in this book may have changed since publication and
may no longer be valid. The views expressed in this work are solely those
of the author and do not necessarily reflect the views of the publisher,
and the publisher hereby disclaims any responsibility for them.

ISBN: 978-1-4525-4284-3 (sc)
ISBN: 978-1-4525-4285-0 (e)

The author of this book does not dispense medical advice or prescribe the use
of any technique as a form of treatment for physical, emotional, or medical
problems without the advice of a physician, either directly or indirectly. The
intent of the author is only to offer information of a general nature to help
you in your quest for emotional and spiritual well-being. In the event you use
any of the information in this book for yourself, which is your constitutional
right, the author and the publisher assume no responsibility for your actions.

Printed in the United States of America

Balboa Press rev. date: 11/17/2011

For my children: Melissa, Jonathan, and Christopher.

May these words bring you comfort and
guidance when you need them. You are the
source of my greatest joy and inspiration.

Inspirations

Purpose

Your soul yearns to fulfill its purpose in life- to express your true self. At some point in our lives we begin to wonder just what the purpose is. We ask these questions within ourselves, "Why am I here?" and "What am I supposed to be doing?" It is when people feel they have no purpose in life, or when they are trying to fulfill someone else's belief of what their purpose should be, they tend to struggle with feelings of depression and low self-esteem.

Let's begin with the question, "What purpose have I given my life?" This goes back to the idea of cause and effect. When we ask ourselves "What purpose have I given my life?" we are then on the cause end of the cause and effect process, instead of the other way around.

Consider your work, personal life and beliefs, and review the steps that got you to this point. If these aspects of life fill you with energy, it is a sign that they are vital to your soul's purpose. However, if any of them make you feel tired, depressed, or even ill, you need to change them.

Sit quietly with this idea for a few minutes without judging yourself. Let your thoughts explore your heart then make a list of all the things that you would love to do. Start by doing the smallest one, and work your way through the list. As you spend time following your heart, you will attract positive energy that will help bring your dreams to fruition!

Every one of us has the ability to have a positive affect on our own lives and on those around us, most especially if we are true to our own purpose.

Love

Nothing is more powerful than love. In this world, there are basically two emotions: love, and fear. Love drives compassion, kindness, acceptance, healing, and unity. It gives us self-esteem, and allows us to esteem others in a healthy way. Fear drives everything that is destructive and creates division.

Jesus taught us that the greatest commandment is to love the Lord our God with all our heart, soul, and mind, and to love our neighbor as ourselves. If we understand this at the deepest level, everything falls into place.

Love is action. Sometimes when our ego gets in the way, we believe love to be just an emotion that requires it to be returned. The greatest love is love without strings or expectation.

An interesting thing about love is that when we give it, more love is generated within us. If we do not love ourselves, it is impossible to love others. Remember always that those who are the least loveable are those who need love the most.

Let us love one another.

Prayer

Prayer is a fundamental element of all belief systems, and all forms of worship. It is both life giving and life changing. It was when I learned to approach life with an attitude of affirmative prayer that my life began to change for the better. Affirmative prayer is not manipulation, it is deeply knowing and trusting the power of God.

Many people tell me that they don't know God, nor do they know how to pray to a god that they do not understand. Although I believe that truly understanding God is beyond human comprehension, I will try to explain what I believe God to be. God is the male/female creative energy of all that is, ever has been, or ever will be. Each of us are part of that powerful creative energy! As I heard a Baptist preacher say some thirty years ago, "Now if that doesn't set you on fire, well then, your wood must be wet!"

A lot of times we say that we believe, but we doubt that we are "good enough" for God's blessings. We believe somehow we have messed up so much that we are beyond reconciliation. I remember my sponsor Lily used to tell me, "If God is for you, then no one can be against you, not even yourself." At first I thought, "yeah, but if you only knew…." Then I began to realize that God did KNOW! Not only did God know all about *me, God wanted my best. God wanted to bless even me! My mess-ups were not what interested God. My wholeness is what interests God, as does yours.*

Affirmative prayer is a step beyond belief. It is communion with God, the creative life-giving energy. It is the knowing, without question, that we can and will be whole. It is knowing that without a doubt, whatever happens in life, the situation holds a blessing and a lesson for us, if we will but see it.

Although there is not one specific "correct" way to pray, nor is there a wrong way to pray, there is a formula that may help you get started. I call it ASK. Begin with Acknowledging God as the creative life giving energy and that you are part of that wonderful energy. Next is Supplication: let your requests be made known to God. Last of all: Know. Know that God's desire is for your best, and that your prayers will be answered accordingly.

Remember ASK.
Acknowledge, Supplication, Know.
Now, let us pray!

Courage

It takes courage to make lifestyle changes. It would be nice if we could "just say no." But, as we all know, it isn't that easy. This is especially true if we are talking about addictive behaviors, which come in a variety of styles, shapes, and sizes.

Typically, the behavior we need to change brought us pleasure or comfort before it brought us pain. Our brain has a mechanism that remembers the pleasure, but tends to minimize or forget the pain. So, when a trigger happens that sets off anxiety or discomfort, our brain returns to the memory of the behavior that brought pleasure or comfort. This "comforting" behavior could manifest itself as compulsive eating, alcohol, sex, shopping or even anger and rage. If we have developed an addiction, we will continue the behavior until it brings us pain again.

We have to learn is new, more effective means of coping that sometimes gets us out of our comfort zone. It takes honesty, awareness, repetition, and commitment to make these changes. But, it can be done!

On a deeper level, we must change our view of ourselves. This takes courage too. At the heart of addiction is a great deal of fear, shame, and guilt. As our addictions take on a life of their own, so does our self-loathing. In order to heal, we must *learn to love and honor ourselves. We must treat ourselves with compassion and respect. It takes courage to see our goodness when we have been programmed to see our imperfections.*

If you are struggling with an addiction or two, or you love someone who is, take courage. Miracles happen everyday! I have heard it said that courage is being fearful, but doing it anyway. This makes sense when making lifestyle changes. Keep in mind: an addiction is what you have, not who you are. There is so much more to you than that! Go ahead, it's okay to look at your good stuff! Trust the process, one day at a time.

Peace

Many people today are drawn to a personal quest for peace. Whether you are drawn to work toward world peace, or you simply want to bring more peace to your neighborhood or family, the quest for peace is a noble one.

Sometimes it feels as if we live in tumultuous times. There are wars and violence all around us. Alcohol and drug abuse is a worldwide epidemic, and all of us have been affected on some level. The divorce rate is higher than ever. We hear constantly about the rate of unemployment and the difficult economy. If this is what we focus on, this is what we will continue to create. Let us be part of the solution. Let peace begin with each of us.

The best way to allow peace to manifest in our lives is to lead by example. Whether by fostering good relationships between people, being at peace with nature, or taking practical action to benefit the world around you; you can be an instrument of peace.

I think of the words of Jesus when he was calming the rough waters, he simply said, "Peace, be still." We can learn from this example when we apply it to the anxiousness within our heart and soul. When we get into compulsive worry, we can reflect on the words "Peace, be still." When we are at peace, we bring peacefulness to the world around us. Difficult situations become easier to manage, and lose their power over us.

My favorite scripture is Proverbs 46:10: "Be still and know that I am God." When I allow this simple affirmation to be infused into my heart, my soul, and my very being, I am filled with peace and bring peace to each situation I encounter.

Have a Peaceful Day!

Respect

Respect is perhaps one of the most desired, yet misunderstood values that we have. Lack of respect for self or others is the cause of most of the inner and outer turmoil we experience in our lives.

We sometimes believe that in order for us to give respect, the other person must earn it. In reality this limits our responsibility. This type of thinking gives other people power and control in our lives.

Respect, like love, is a choice. We do not have to like or agree with another person's behavior in order to show them respect. Each person has the right to walk their individual path and experience the necessary bumps along the way in order to achieve soul growth. Showing respect to others is a reflection of us, not them.

When we have self-respect, we will naturally have appropriate boundaries in our relationships with others. The great law of karma is that the energy that we give out is the energy that is returned to us. This law is taught among all religious and philosophical belief systems.

When we have self-respect we will recognize, love, and honor our gifts, talents, and abilities. With self- respect, we will no *longer indulge in self-defeating beliefs or harmful behavior. With self-respect and respect of others, we rise to our highest potential in all areas of our lives.*

Forgiveness

*A*s a daily practice it is wise to search our thoughts to see if we have shut anyone outside of our hearts. If, in this practice, we discover resentment or hurt, let us open our heart and mind to forgiveness.

Allow the breath of God to fill you with compassion. With each breath, be filled with love and peace. As you think of those you wish to forgive, or if you recognize feelings of hurt or pain that keep you stuck in resentment, allow yourself to recognize in their reflection the same Spirit that is in you.

At this level of spiritual knowing, understand that we are all one in God. Release the judgments of worldly thoughts and allow forgiveness to unite us in love.

Sometimes forgiveness is really difficult, especially when it feels like darts are flying all around you. It hurts when someone has perhaps unjustly judged you or attacked your character due to misunderstanding. Perhaps there are issues within yourself that must be addressed.

Addictions of all kinds are self-destructive and are characterized with shame. This includes the addiction of controlling others. Shame is what separates us from God and from others. Guilt can motivate us to make necessary changes. Shame is different.

Shame gives us the illusion that we are flawed. When we feel flawed as human beings we develop defensive behaviors that push others away.

Sometimes we have the mistaken belief that if we forgive others, we are somehow approving of behavior that has been hurtful or destructive.

Look at your motives; look deeply within your heart. Ask God to help you achieve pureness of heart, honestly. Allow God's healing, loving energy to fill your being. Then take that God-consciousness and forgive others. No longer dwell on your pain, but purposely focus loving energy on any thoughts that separate you from the Divine.

Forgive yourself and forgive others. This is the way to peace of mind.

Joy

J oy is not merely an emotion; it is a way of being. To experience joy is to experience calm, non-attachment. Attachment to the way things "should be" or to a certain outcome implies that anything outside of that mindset is wrong or unacceptable.

When in a state of joy, or non-attachment, to a certain way of seeing things, we have room to open our minds and hearts and experience life in a new way. Instead of seeing things from a black or white perspective, we begin to see life with a multiplicity of color. Experiences become rich and full in a state of joy!

Joy is abiding in the understanding that all is as it should be, even if I don't understand it!

Joy is knowing deeply that even through difficult situations there is opportunity for growth and wisdom. This applies on a personal, social, and even global level.

Joy opens us to the opportunity to give and to receive love, which of course, is our greatest need and desire in life.

Joy allows us to genuinely experience the I AM, which is unity with all that is, ever was, or ever shall be.

Have a joyful day!

Eternity

There have been many books written, songs sung, and works of art created for the purpose of reflecting the significance of mankind. Yet, sometimes we doubt the significance of our role in the magnificent web of life. We have a tendency to narrow the importance of our existence to the amount of years between the date of our birth and the date of our death. We tend to think in terms of eternity beginning when we die and existing somewhere "out there", and if we are good enough and in favor of God, we will get there, someday.

I have a secret for you. You are in eternity, right here, right now! Every breath you breathe, every thought you think, every experience you have is significant. When you were created, you were created in the likeness, image, and essence of God. This means that you carry a bit of the Divine with you everywhere you go, all of the time. This is true of everyone. When you truly understand this truth, it will change how you see yourself and how you see others.

This also means that you have enormous power in how you create your experience of life. Every situation, no matter how painful or difficult, has a gift and a lesson for us. Every experience holds an opportunity for acceptance, love, and personal growth. Sometimes this personal growth comes in the form of learning forgiveness, tolerance, and the acceptance of differences.

Everything you think, say, and do has a rippling effect on the world. Consider how an act of love or kindness can change a person's disposition, and then in turn they respond to others with kindness verses anger. This is energy in motion. Think about when you are in victim mentality and how when you nurse those ideas, you bring the energy of resentment and bitterness to your environment and to your relationships with others. How different is it when we bring love and acceptance verses anger and resentment?

Release

Release any thoughts of doubt, fear, or ideas of lack, and lean into the understanding that you are an integral part of the Divine Universe. Within the universe there is plenty of everything for everyone. As we let go of fear and doubt, we naturally disperse the gifts of God appropriately.

Breathe deeply, as every cell of your body is infused with the knowledge that the desire of the creator is for your highest good, and that prosperity begins with trusting in this understanding.

Let go of doubt and fear. Recognize that the past has had its purpose of teaching you about patience, tolerance, and grace. Be at peace with the passage of time. See clearly that each stage of life has its lessons and its gifts, and joyously accept both.

With appreciation of life's lessons, release the past and stand firmly in the present moment.

Release any fear, and accept without doubt that you are in unity with the Absolute. Understand that fear, doubt, and lack are created by the mindset of division. When we understand that we are united with all of life, we experience ease in giving and receiving.

Contemplate and accept deeply the truth that the spirit of God is not fear, but peace, power, and a sound mind. Since God is love, and love is the opposite of fear; let go of fear, and you will become love itself.

Soul Food

*T*here are different aspects of our existence that must be nourished. How we feel physically has a great deal to do with how we nourish and take care of our body. If we feed it a bunch of toxins, and lay around and do nothing, our body will have depleted energy and will feel bad. We need life-giving food and exercise for physical health.

Spiritual health has to do with reaching up and out, to something bigger and higher than ourselves. Some people see this as God, while some people see it as a Higher Power, or even Humanity as a whole.

Our soul is the part of us that governs our relationship with everything else. It is the life force within us. The health of our soul is our moral compass, and must be nurtured as well. When our spiritual self looks up and out, our soul self looks within.

If we constantly take in negativity, violence, and anger, this is what our soul will reflect. In other words, what we think in our mind is how we relate to ourselves and to the world. As we feed our physical self a healthy diet, so must we feed our soul life-giving food!

Soul food can come in different forms. Holy books, such as the Bible, the Tao Te Ching, and good literature have a wealth of food for the soul. Try taking a walk in nature and be mindful *of the beauty around you. Spend some time in prayer and meditation each day and see the difference in your life and in your relationships!*

Enjoy some soul food today and everyday!

Divine Design

Made in the image, likeness, and essence of God, we human beings have the capacity to design and create through our spiritual, mental, and physical capabilities. Each one of us is an artist, a creator at our core, designing and weaving the fabric of our lives. When we live our lives in cooperation with the Divine and our Highest Self, our capabilities are limitless.

We are born with free will to create our lives any way we choose. When we have a limited view of ourselves and our connection with the Universe, we are unable to see our true potential. In fact, what we create in our lives is parallel to our belief system. When we open our heart and mind and tap into the energy of God, there is no limit to the good that we can create!

We each have unique skills and strengths. One person may create a brilliant computer program; another, a stunning work of art; and yet another, a harmonious home with children who feel loved and worthy. The ways in which we create are endless. May we all share our beautiful gifts with the world.

Reflection

Time spent in reflection is like a retreat from the busyness of the day. Take time from daily activities to consider some of the blessings in your life.

Take comfort in how supported you have felt on life's journey so far, even when things were difficult. Consider the love of family and friends, as well as the ever-present energy of God.

Ponder how best to share the love that you are, and reflect on what you might do to make a difference in another's life. Pray for strength, comfort, and restoration for our fellow travelers.

Sit with questions that arise and allow the answers to unfold on their own. Know instinctively that the answers to life's most difficult questions lie within you, as that is where the spirit of God resides.

As you think about your day, remind yourself to be fully in the moment. Let go of any worries about the future or regrets of the past. Look around and appreciate the gifts of your life and the blessings of the journey thus far.

Enjoy quiet time in reflection and remember to appreciate the many ways God shows up in your life. When you are consciously aware, you see the Divine reflected in the eyes of a new acquaintance, in the song of Spring, and in the stirrings of your soul.

Spend a few moments in quiet reflection and gratitude each day. You will see the blessings of your life become crystal clear!

Kaleidoscope

There are many life lessons to consider when looking into a kaleidoscope. Kaleidoscopes show us how different shapes, sizes, colors, and nuances create beautiful changing patterns, just as in our life experiences.

I have a beautiful kaleidoscope on my desk that was a gift from my husband. The barrel is made of polished maple. The patterns that it creates are made by different colored rocks floating in oil. I find it very relaxing to gaze into it.

I often have clients pick up the kaleidoscope and look through it when they are struggling with making necessary changes in their lives. I ask them to point it towards the light and gently rotate it. As it rotates, the rocks float in the oil, changing their order and pattern, displaying elegant and unique mandalas. I explain to them that this represents life. Little changes can make big differences! All experiences are unique, different, and necessary for our personal growth.

Imagine how dull the world would be if there were only one color, idea, or taste! Life would become stagnant and dull. It is that which we resist that creates the pain in our lives.

> "Life is a process of becoming, a
> combination of states we have
> to go through. Where people fail

is that they wish to elect a state
and remain in it. This is a kind of
death."

Anias Nin

Besides the necessity of change and the abundance of possibilities, the kaleidoscope teaches us is to point towards the light. It is the light that allows the kaleidoscope to display its brilliance. When we point towards our Divine Source and are infused with the power of God, which is indeed genuine love for all of creation, we can embrace change and differences with love and power instead of with pain and resistance.

Consider the possibilities!

Thunderstorms

Sometimes life gives us mental, physical, and emotional thunderstorms. These storms may come in the form of illness, difficult decisions, divorce, financial strain, or the death of loved ones. None of us get through life without a storm or two. Although these storms always leave us with a gift of greater insight or improved inner strength, they are not enjoyable to experience.

Sometimes storms are huge, and leave us with no other option but to figure out how to survive it. I am always amazed when natural disasters have occurred how the human spirit comes together to help one another through prayer, physical help, or whatever is needed. Huge storms force us to stop and consider what is truly important in life.

At times during life's storms, I may feel unsure and in need of clarity and guidance. Perhaps I have an important decision in front of me, and I need to discern my next steps.

Wherever I am, God is, so I know there is clear direction available. I open my spiritual ears and listen. Guidance comes in clear and unmistakable ways; a divine idea, a new perspective, or even a seeming coincidence may lead the way.

When I seek inner guidance, I open my mind and heart to Spirit. I act on the divine direction I receive, which leaves me *feeling relieved, confident, and more aware of my Inner Guide. No matter how daunting the storm may seem, I know I will get through it, even if it means that I transition from this life to the next.*

Grace

Grace has been defined as the state of kindness and favor towards someone, often with a focus on a benefit given to the object. Divine grace is given freely, without having been earned. If this were not so, it would not be grace. This definition gives us a great deal to consider.

We often ask for Divine grace when dealing with difficult situations, and indeed this is an appropriate thing to do. We are told that there is nothing that can remove us from the love and grace of God. There is in fact only one thing that can separate us from union with Divine grace, and that is our ego.

We like the idea of being "gracious," but are we gracious when others fall out of our favor, or when they disagree with our religious or political points of view? Are we gracious to people of other races, sexual orientation, or culture? Are we gracious to those we love when they fail to meet our expectations?

Grace has the ability to heal broken hearts, families, and even nations. Every spiritual belief system teaches the great law of karma, or sowing and reaping. In other words, the energy we give is the energy that returns. The grace we give is the grace we will receive. But, grace is not grace if it is given expecting something in return. It is only grace if it is given freely.

Grace is most difficult given to oneself. Our ego tells us that sin, or missing the mark, requires punishment. Our ego has the ability to keep us lost and stuck in self-pity and self-destruction. Our ego also has the ability to allow us to criticize and judge others. Without grace, there is no reconciliation. With grace, all things move into a place of wholeness and balance. When in a state of grace, we focus on the essence of the Divine in ourselves and in others.

It is easy for us to reflect on the idea of grace and see it as truth. Our ego tells us that there are exceptions to the rule. There are no exceptions to the law of grace.

Our world needs grace. Let us be gracious, one to another!

Truth

The truth is we are meant to live a life of wholeness, happiness, and peace. We are to work in harmony with our environment and with humanity. When you listen to the words around you, it is easy to believe that the truth is division, judgment, and exclusion. It is easy to begin to believe that the "truth" is that others are out to get us and everything is falling apart.

The truth is that what we focus on is what we create in our reality. This truth is what Jesus meant when he told us that he came so that we might have life and have it abundantly.

I consciously release any misconceptions that have limited my thinking and being in the world. Spirit in me reveals Truth to my soul.

I speak Truth to my body with affirmations of health and wholeness. As I contemplate my home and workplace, my friendships and family, I affirm the Truth of harmony and prosperity.

Truth is unchanging. It is love, peace, health, and eternal goodness. As I contemplate my life through the lens of Truth, I do so with thanksgiving. Thank you, God, for the eternal Truth, everywhere present, revealed in prayer and expressed through me.

Your Inner Castle

Somehow along the way we have come to believe that we are separate and different from each other. We believe that we are divided by our race, culture, or our religious and political beliefs. The truth is that separateness is an illusion. We are all connected in this great web of life!

The things I admire in others are a reflection of what I admire in myself. Likewise, the things I despise in others are aspects I deny in myself. Until we are able to honestly embrace all facets of ourselves as being part of our life curriculum, we cannot change or improve those things.

Visualize your heart as a young child. Your heart was like a beautiful castle with many rooms that you loved to explore. You enjoyed going into your rooms experiencing the beauty and uniqueness in them all. Then as life went along, others came along and told you, "Your room is not like mine, you need to close that door and not go inside." You got this message from many different people, and you came to believe that your rooms had to look like everyone else's until you closed so many doors that your castle began to resemble a two room house in need of repair.

Today, go into your castle and open the doors! Enjoy and embrace all aspects of yourself and your beliefs, and allow others to do the same. You will find that what you feared is not all *that daunting. When we are able to love who we are, we are able to nurture ourselves back to wholeness. When we are able to honestly embrace ourselves, we no longer need the defensive behaviors that led to pain, suffering and separateness. We are able to experience our inner castle.*

Today, be happy being you!

Day Dreaming

My work, and indeed everything that I do, is an expression of who I am, as I use my mind, physical capabilities, and actions to create something of value in the world. It doesn't really matter what my particular "job" is, it matters more what I bring to it. If I am content, peaceful, and joyful within myself, I will bring this attitude to whatever it is that I do.

I realize that I do my best work when I am relaxed and refreshed.

I take time for myself today to daydream the possibilities for good. Closing my eyes and opening my imagination, I feel great hope inside. As I dream of my life's potential, I become aware that I have been given many talents to use, many gifts from Spirit. I resolve to use these gifts to see my dreams come true.

When I return to work after giving myself time to relax and dream, I feel nurtured and revitalized. I am able to see beyond any limitations I may have imposed upon myself.

I feel peaceful and inspired knowing that if I can dream something; I have the ability to create it.

Take time to dream today, and see the endless possibilities!

Listen

When considering the most important components to a good relationship, most people will agree that communication is at the top of the list. What people are typically saying is that they want to feel valuable to the other person. We feel valued when we feel heard.

The most important aspect of all communication is listening. When we genuinely listen to others, we are saying without words, "I value what you think and feel." Very often when we are trying to communicate with others, we are busy thinking about how we are going to respond, before the other person is ever finished with what they are saying. When we do not listen, and when we interrupt, we are trying to dominate or overpower the conversation.

Consider for a moment how the world would change, if for one day, everyone would genuinely listen to what others were trying to say. If we would genuinely listen from the heart, without preconceived ideas and judgments, we would begin to see things much more clearly. If we would listen to our brothers and sisters from the heart, we would be practicing brotherly love as Jesus taught us to do.

Jimi Hendrix, whom some of remember as one of the greatest guitar players of all time, said it well when he said, "Only when *the power of love overcomes the love of power, the world will know peace."*

Let's consider for a moment the scripture in Proverbs that says, "Be still, and know that I AM God." This implies listening at the deepest level. When we learn to listen at this level, we will honor and esteem our own intuition. Our intuition is the voice of God within. When we learn this principle, we will learn to genuinely listen to and value others.

Today, genuinely listen.

Passion

Passion is that wonderful energy that feeds the soul! It gives life and energy to the pursuit of our most cherished ideas and dreams. Passion makes us feel excitement and joy. Passion brings color to our lives and to our relationships! Without passion, our endeavors become listless and mundane.

Like fire, passion must be handled wisely. Our passions must be channeled to our greatest good and to the good of others, or else it can become destructive.

When I understand my connection to the Divine and accept my vital place in humanity, I trust in my instincts and in my creative abilities! I bring passion to everything that I do. When my passions are channeled for my highest good and for the good of others, nothing is impossible!

Ask yourself, what do I love? What makes my heart sing? Take a risk and follow your heart song, with passion. Amazing things will happen!

Relationships

We are all in relationship with other people. We may not be in a romantic relationship, but we are in relationship with everyone we interact with. How we interact with others is directly related with how we interact with ourselves.

Our most basic need in life is to love and be loved. If we do not love ourselves, it is not just difficult to love others, it is impossible. Loving ourselves begins with two basic concepts. The first requirement to being a healthy self is to be authentic. This means being comfortable in your own skin and being true to yourself. When we are authentic we have a peaceful and centered attitude. This energy flows from us and affects everyone around us in a positive way. Be happy being you!

The second requirement to loving ourselves is to accept our sacredness. When we really understand that we are made of the essence of God, we can no longer treat ourselves with loathing and disrespect, nor do we allow it from others. When we take this a step further and understand that others are made of the same essence, we can no longer treat them with disrespect. We begin treating others with unconditional positive regard.

Look in the mirror. Look deeply for a minute or two. Do you see that sacred person in your eyes? If not, continue looking. Look beyond the imperfections of the body and the skin. Look directly *into your eyes. Look beyond the perceived mistakes that you have made and look beyond any judgment you have of yourself and you will see wisdom and love in its purest form.*

Now take this reflection of love and give it to everyone you encounter today.

Words

Words are very powerful things! The words we speak have the power to heal a broken heart, encourage and esteem others, give strength, and give life to imagination! How powerful are words? We are taught in the book of Genesis that God spoke and the world was created!

Words also have the power to break hearts, destroy relationships, and create all kinds of havoc in this world. The book of James counsels us that words are like a match thrown into a forest; as words can destroy a person, a tiny spark can overtake the forest.

Let us choose our words wisely when speaking to others, as what comes out of our mouth is a reflection of our soul. When we watch the media, we see all around us fear, hurt, and pain. Let us exhort one another to goodness! Let us be a healing presence in this world.

As we give advice to others, let us first look within and consider our motive. Are we coming from a place of ego, or a place of genuine love and concern? Before speaking, it is wise to ask ourselves, "Does this need to be said? Does this need to be said by me? Does this need to be said now?"

Let your words bring peace to your life!

Intention

I live my life with intention, trusting in Divine outcome. This moves me from a place of belief to KNOWING that everything is in divine order.

When I live my life from a point of intention, I consciously create my experiences. If I expect a joyful encounter, I receive a joyful encounter. If I see my day going smoothly, I create such a day. By setting my intention, I am determining what my life will look like each day.

This does not mean difficult situations won't occur, it just means I change my relationship to them. When difficulties occur I will instinctively know how to handle them and will not get all caught up in the drama. I view challenges as opportunities for practicing compassion and for personal growth.

I set my intention and let go of the outcome. I infuse my intentions with love, peace and understanding, knowing that God is my Source and all is well.

Intend a beautiful day!

Important verses Urgent

It is so easy to get caught up in the fast pace and urgency of daily life to the point we miss the most important aspects of our life. The areas that seem to be affected the most are our health, our relationships, and our spiritual life. Many of us have become overly focused on work, a toxic relationship, or even an addiction, truly thinking that we were doing the right thing. We then awaken, so to speak, and wonder where all the time went.

There are situations that arise that cause us to stop and give all of our attention to the immediate issue. This may come in the form of illness that lays us flat, the death of a loved one, or a natural disaster. These difficult situations hold the gift of teaching us what is most important as human beings.

In all religious practices, we are taught the importance of taking time aside to realign with ourselves and with our Source. In Christianity this is described as the Sabbath. In the Ten Commandments we are taught to remember the Sabbath and to keep it holy. This means to set apart. The Sabbath was not meant to be a stressful day of go, go, go, it was meant to be a day of rest and reflection. Many eastern religions teach the importance of meditation as a way of uniting with the Absolute. Even in nature we see the necessity of rest for regeneration. Bears hibernate and plants go dormant and come back stronger and healthier the next season.

Today, and everyday, I will take time aside to care for myself and to align myself with God. In this way I will have the strength, wisdom, and peace of mind to handle what the experience of life gives me. I know that when I take care of the important things in life, urgent situations lose their power to unsettle me and are taken care of more easily.

Get into the Flow!

Flow: a lovely word that immediately conjures up a vision of a free, unrestricted entity, like water. Water finds its own level naturally, so flow means the natural awareness of where I come to rest in the scheme of this universe; my natural fit so to speak. As the world around me changes, I shift without resistance to my next natural fit.

When I let go of resistance and just let life happen the way it is supposed to, I get into the flow of the energy of the Universe. When I am in the flow, my creative power is limitless. I am not constricted by resistant thoughts that come from fear, doubt, or the worry of non-acceptance. I am free to be me.

Being in the flow is when I stop forcing or trying to make something happen. Things naturally start falling into place, and often things that I could not even imagine begin to unfold. When I stop trying to control the uncontrollable, change the past, or define the path that my loved ones choose, I am free to love, accept, and forgive.

Addiction is resistance. It is a compulsive desire to change or alter the way we feel. Being stuck in an addiction to drugs, alcohol, self-pity, anger, or the need to control is like swimming upstream against the current. It makes you tired! When we can observe our emotions without judging them or without trying *to alter them, they lose power over us, and we become unstuck. We get into the flow of life!*

When we stop resisting life naturally just works out the way it is supposed to. What we once perceived as difficult situations now become part of the river of life.

Get into the flow!

Live Your Truth!

So what is our truth? Our truth is our authenticity. We were born in a state of love and acceptance of others and ourselves. We were born wise. As babies, we did not understand fear, prejudice, poor self-esteem, or resentments. These manifestations are learned behaviors that come from dealing with life experiences and from unconscious people.

The truth is that life will sometimes hand you difficult situations. It is your choice to grow in wisdom and love when faced with challenges, or to become defined by them and live your life in victim stance.

Notice your suffering and explore it so that you can learn from it. You can choose to stop being absorbed by your negative emotions and let go of your story as a victim. Claim your birthright as a wise and courageous person who makes good decisions, who doesn't run from pain but instead walks through it in order to learn the hidden lessons that adversity offers. Turn your life into the soil that grows beautiful flowers in life. Put away your fear and allow your creativity to shine.

Several years ago Leann Womack came out with a song called "I Hope You Dance." This song resonated with my soul. When my son married his wife five years ago, it was to this song that I danced with him at his wedding as he created his new life as a *man and a husband. It was my desire for him to live his truth, and dance with life.*

When we get caught up in ego and addictions, in actuality we are running from our truth. Our ego will create defensive and controlling behavior and the illusion of division. Our addictions to anger, resentment, and substances are an attempt to keep us from feeling vulnerable, which keeps us from experiencing intimacy with others.

Let go of the fear that what you say doesn't matter, because it does! Trust in your creative force. If you want to paint, paint! If you want to sing, sing! Living your truth will feed your soul. Your truth is based on love, even if you have forgotten.

Our Stories

*E*ach day of our life we are creating our life story. For some years I was unhappy with my story. I had a tendency to focus on the perceived mistakes I had made and on my "character defects". At that time, loving who I was and loving my life did not come naturally or easily.

Then, I began listening to other people's stories. I read of people who had overcome trials and difficulties. People such as, Helen Keller, Victor Frankl, and many others who had made the most of their life circumstances and used their adversity to make a positive impact on humanity inspired me. I learned that each part of my life, even the painful parts, have taught me valuable lessons. The most important lesson has been compassion for others and myself.

People suffer losses, celebrate victories, and make life-changing decisions. I learn from their stories. As a counselor I have the unique experience of coaching others to make positive changes in their lives. I see them face their pain, overcome obstacles and recreate their stories. It is a joy to share in the journey of transformation!

In the same way, I tell my own story by the way I live and by the choices I make. My story may be one of courage, of kindness, or of creativity. Perhaps my life inspires others to greater achievement. Each day of my life, I add a page to my story. If I want to begin a fresh chapter, I am free to begin anew.

I begin each day eager to see what will happen on this page of my journey!

Embrace your story and write it as you wish it to be.

Paradigm Shift

One of the most difficult teachings in scripture for people to understand is when we are encouraged by Jesus to turn the other cheek. We are left with thoughts such as "Do I just stand there and let someone beat me up?" "Do I live with no boundaries?" "Do we just let others overtake us?"

In his wonderful book Sermon on the Mount, *Emmet Fox explains that the instruction about turning the other cheek refers to changing one's thought when faced with error, changing from the error to the Truth- and as a rule, it works like magic. If someone is behaving badly, instead of thinking about how bad they are, immediately switch your attention from the human to the Divine. Concentrate upon God, or upon the Real Spiritual Self of the person in question. You will find if you really do this that his or her behavior will immediately change. This is the secret to handling difficult people, and Jesus understood it thoroughly.*

Now, let's take this idea a step further to the understanding "Where our thoughts go, energy flows." Sometimes we get stuck in a certain way of thinking. This is called a paradigm. Paradigms of thought can control our life! For instance, if I constantly think "I don't want to get hurt." I will be focusing on being hurt. I will be fearful and distrustful of others. Therefore, I will set up all kinds of walls and defenses that keep me from experiencing intimacy, joy, and open, honest communication. If instead I think, "I deserve to be happy and have good relationships in my life," I will be more open and I will be able to see the good in others and in myself. I will have more appropriate boundaries because I see the good in myself. I attract into my life what I see in myself.

Likewise, if I focus on "I don't want to relapse" or "I don't want to use drugs" I am focusing on relapse and relapse is more likely to happen. Instead, if I shift the paradigm to "I want to be healthy and I want to feel good." My attention will move to healthier ways of living.

Today and everyday, focus on what you do want, and not on what you don't want. Remember, where your thoughts go, energy flows!

Prosperity

We live in an abundant universe. This means that there is plenty of everything we need, provided we are good stewards of our planet and our resources.

When we give freely, not only of our financial resources, but also of our time, energy, and love, we prosper. When we share from our willingness and eagerness to bless others, we are blessed. This is the great law of karma, or sowing and reaping.

Whether we recycle gently used household items, spend time tutoring a child, or volunteer to assist someone in need, we are giving from the heart. Giving can come in the form of a kind word of encouragement, a smile, or even positive thoughts about others. We receive the blessings of joy, satisfaction, and gratitude as soon as we give to others.

As we give and receive from the heart, we realize that material possessions do not define prosperity. Prosperity is a mindset, a consciousness or deep knowing that everything we need is already supplied.

Giving of our heart opens the way for blessings to circulate. Let us give one to another.

Renew Your Energy

Sometimes the tasks of daily life scatter our energy, and we feel confused and drained. At times like these it helps to take a moment and refuel.

When my car needs gas, I refuel the tank. When my faith needs refueling, I pause and pray. I sit in silent meditation, allowing the strength and peace of Spirit to fill me. Praying renews my faith and gives me the power to move forward.

Sometimes I take a few minutes to do some slow meditative yoga poses, which slows down my obsessive thoughts and helps me to refocus. I go for a walk and appreciate the beauty that is all around me that I tend to miss when I get caught up in the everyday rush of life.

I say a prayer of thanksgiving for the divine mystery of life. God is as near to me as my breath, and yet beyond understanding. Communion with God through prayer and meditation is all the fuel I need. It fills me with the assurance that all is well.

Renewed and ready to set out in the right direction, I take the next step on my divine path.

Take some time to refuel, and have a great day!

The Journey

Life's journey takes us down many roads, and progress can be measured by various mileposts or accomplishments. Although our accomplishments are fulfilling and give us many opportunities, the real lessons and gifts come from our experiences along the way.

The journey is more meaningful than any one outcome or destination. Every moment is special and of great value. Every realization is another step towards spiritual growth.

Many people come to counseling feeling as if their life has been a failure due to past mistakes, broken relationships, and emotional hurts. But, this is not so. Young or old, there is something to be learned from each person and situation we experience. Every day is a new day, and a new opportunity. We cannot change the past, nor should we want to. What we can change is our view of the past. Along life's journey we can change our regrets into compassion for others and ourselves.

The journey gives us many opportunities to make meaningful connections with our fellow travelers. This is what life is really all about.

Each day brings me closer to self-realization and closer to God. As I remain centered in God's presence, my journey may not always be easy, but it is safe and sacred.

Embrace the journey!

Wisdom

Wisdom is recognizing and accepting what we can and cannot change, and allowing our suffering to teach us about ourselves and about life.

We can know all the facts and information in the world, but if we don't know how to apply the information in a positive and effective way, we do not have wisdom. Life is filled with mysteries, and we don't always have the answers to certain questions. Wisdom allows us to see that there are things outside of our control, and to be at peace with that.

Wisdom gives us the courage to do what is difficult and to make the changes necessary for healing to occur. Wisdom is what helps us transform the way we think, feel, and behave. Sometimes wisdom is letting go of trying to control certain situations in our lives and in the lives of others and allowing the natural consequences, or karma, to work.

It is inspiring to hear about people who have triumphed over difficulties or recovered from addictions or other destructive habits. Wise people no longer define themselves by their past or re-tell the story of their suffering and misery. Instead, they tell the story of acceptance of life on life's terms, love of others and new possibilities.

Breathe!

Deep conscious breathing is the cornerstone of health! It lowers our blood pressure, slows down our heart rate, relives stress, and infuses us with life-giving energy.

Approximately 65 percent of our body is oxygen. It fuels our brain, refreshes our blood cells, and supplies us with energy. This oxygen is the very breath of Spirit--breathed into us, providing life.

Breathing is inherent, yet it also works in tandem with the conscious mind. With every breath, we are renewed and rejuvenated. With every breath, we have the opportunity to be aware of the spirit of God.

As I inhale, I breathe in goodness, life and peace. My entire being vibrates with the power and presence of the Divine within me. With each exhale, I release the toxins of worry, fear, and doubt, allowing positive energy and truth to fill the space.

Deep breathing fills us with Peace, Power and A Sound Mind!

Affirmation

Affirmation is a means of bringing us into a state of serenity and balance. Affirmations, or mantras, are not about changing reality, but about changing our relationship to the circumstances in our lives. Difficult situations sometimes happen, but how we react to them is our choice.

Affirmations have a powerful effect on our psyche. Affirmations come from and reinforce our belief system. In other words, our thoughts create our reality. This is not a new fad or New Age concept. Mantras and affirmations have been used throughout time to reinforce belief systems. Consider beloved prayers we say to help us find peace, or slogans we use in AA meetings to give us strength. Buddhist monks use mantras to help them attain focus. Catholics use mantras in the form of the Rosary to invoke the presence of God.

Affirmations can be positive or negative. If I tell myself long enough that I will be sick, I will be. The stress of that thought will deplete my immune system and I will get sick. If I tell myself I am strong, wise, and capable, I will approach life that way and my life will be easier.

Sometimes our belief systems are so ingrained that we must tell ourselves different information over and over to make that change happen in our psyche. Choose what has meaning for you.

I particularly like the term Namaste. Namaste is a Sanskrit word the means the God spirit in me recognizes and honors the God spirit in you. Namaste is significant because it is a humbling gesture. Namaste is done as recognition that we are all on equal standing; all of us are children of divinity. We are one.

Choose what is significant for you. Repeat it in your heart and mind until it becomes your reality.

Equanimity

When my children were little, one of their favorite stories for me to read to them was <u>Alexander and The Terrible, Horrible, No Good, Very Bad Day</u> by Judith Vorst. In the story, Alexander was a six-year-old boy who had a propensity for making messes and getting into trouble. Alexander thought the answer to his problems was to move to Australia where his days would surely be better. His Mom would always remind him that some days were just like that, even in Australia. This story rings true for most of us. Some days, life just throws you a curve ball or two.

I've learned a secret about getting through those days. It is called equanimity. Equanimity means remaining calm in the face of the storm. When we remain calm, we are able to think clearly and solve problems more easily.. It doesn't mean that life doesn't give us difficult situations; it just means we don't remain in the drama for very long. Typically when little storm clouds come, we work them, worry them, over-think them, and turn them into a hurricane in our minds!

I trust in the Divine Spirit, knowing that everything happening in my life is for my personal growth and higher good, even when it doesn't appear that way. I can get back into equanimity knowing that the answers are within me.

I close my eyes, take a deep breath and let the storm settle. I say to myself, "Ok, this is the situation, now what?" I trust that with the guidance of God within me, I will make the best decisions possible. I have learned through practicing equanimity that what used to seem like monumental issues really are not that big of a deal.

Have a peaceful day!

Agreements

The word agreement means to have an opinion about, or to act in accordance with, an idea or belief that is the same as someone else. We make agreements throughout our lives. Some of them are good, and some of them should be challenged if we are to attain a sense of self worth and authenticity.

We make agreements with our families about our identities. We make agreements with our culture and religious system about what we believe to be true. We make agreements with the rules and regulations of our society in order to maintain order and peace. Of course many of these agreements are necessary to give us structure.

One of our most important needs in life is a sense of belonging. In order to belong, we make certain agreements, sometimes to our detriment. For instance, if I take on the belief as a child that I am not "this enough" or "that enough," I may spend my entire life trying to prove that I am. I may spend a vast amount of energy trying to prove to others and myself that I am smart enough, tough enough, thin enough, pretty enough, or cool enough to be acceptable and loved. The agreement of not being "enough" can lead to all kinds of harmful behaviors, including deadly addictions to drugs, alcohol, anger, criminal behavior, sex, or eating disorders.

Over the years as a therapist I have found that if a person has a sense of shame, which is in reality, the agreement of "not being good enough," it is much easier for them to look at their negative attributes than it is for them to see their goodness. This person may have spent so much time trying to agree with what society thinks they should be that they have become lost to their true nature.

Today, make the agreement to be happy being the person you were created to be! Only when we are true to ourselves can we be at peace. It is through our unique differences and our authenticity that we create the beautiful tapestry of life!

New Beginnings

Every day of my life has the potential to be a new beginning. In fact, each moment has that same potential. There are fresh choices to make, new ideas to adopt, and new creations to bring to life. I trust that our individual and collective potential is limitless!

My life is under my authority, and I use this power to create the life I choose. It is easy to get mired down in past mistakes. Instead, I choose to use the past as a learning experience.

At the start of any new venture, I may worry that it will be too hard or wonder whether I will know what to do. How I choose to respond to these worries is up to me. Sometimes I need to just step aside, take a deep breath, and trust that intuitive direction will come. It always does!

I choose peace, faith, and my God-given ability to succeed. I know that I am the very essence of the living, loving God within me. The indwelling Spirit supports and encourages me to take the next right step. It might just be the start of the most satisfying time of my life!

Harmony

There are times when we are tempted to go along with another's wishes, even though we feel uncomfortable doing so. Just the thought of going against what we believe causes inner conflict. In those moments, it helps to pause and go within to give yourself time to make the choice that is right for you.

Living your life in agreement with your values creates harmony at the depths of your being. Like the clear tone of a bell, waves of harmony go forth from you to bless the people around you. Harmonious vibrations are created.

When we act in accord with our beliefs, we not only create harmony for ourselves, but we also nurture harmony in others.

Always remember, when you are true to yourself, you are being true to others, even if it may not appear that way.

Be in harmony with your principles and your actions!

Witnessing

Witnessing is the ability to step aside and mindfully watch what is going on around you at all times and choose an appropriate response. I call this paying attention on purpose. Learning this skill will profoundly change your life! It moves you from a state of being reactionary and gives you the ability to think and make wise decisions.

It is not typically our actions that get us in trouble, but our reactions! Most of us genuinely know how to treat others well and be respectful. But, sometimes we become stuck in reactions such as anger, sarcasm, or self-pity.

The next time you feel angry, or upset, step back and say to yourself, "There I go feeling angry," or "There I go obsessing about this." Then watch yourself being angry. All feelings are sensations in your body, so notice in your body where you feel it.

Take a deep breath and think, "How would I prefer to see this situation?" "What can I do to help this situation have a better outcome?" Be mindful of how you relate to others.

When we step back and think before we react, we are then in a position to act with integrity.

Be mindful today, and everyday!

The Three Poisons

Mindfulness is the ability to be keenly aware of what is happening all around you in the moment, and to choose an appropriate mental, emotional, and behavioral response. Being mindful gives us the ability to see the beauty in the world and in other people; and to appreciate diversity. Most of all, mindfulness gives us insight into what is going on within ourselves.

The Buddhists have a teaching about the lack of mindfulness. This teaching says that three poisons plague man. The three poisons are aggression, appetite, and, apathy. Three men are sitting on the edge of the Grand Canyon with all of the beauty and splendor before them. The first man is unable to see the incredible beauty because all he can think about is the person who did an injustice to him and how angry he is about it. The second man is unable to see the magnificence of the Grand Canyon because all he can think about is the drink he wishes he had. The third man, plagued by apathy, is like a man with a bag on his head.

Look around you and be mindful of what is there. Look within yourself and be aware of how you are creating your life circumstances, or how you are relating to yourself and others. Instead of focusing on the past, and any injustices that may have been done to you: move into the present. Let go of worrying about what may happen down the road, and be mindful of the opportunities in the present moment.

Choose today to bring mindfulness and appreciation to each situation and see what happens! Be aware of your responses both within and without. We can't control other people, places, and things. We can, however, control how we relate to them. Understand that other people's behavior is about them and not about you.

Remember, it is when people are behaving the least loveable that they need love the most.

Serenity

Serenity is peace of mind, the knowledge that all is as it should be for the greatest good. Serenity comes from a lack of fear. Serenity is a deep calm abiding in the present moment.

I leave serenity when I begin to focus on the past, on resentments, and on regrets.

I leave serenity when I leave the present and become focused on the future and worried about how I am going to create the future money, relationships, and circumstances.

I return to serenity when I let go of grasping and go back to knowing who I am and where I stand with God and with the universe.

I return to serenity when I get out of "What can I gain from the world or from this person or situation?" and return to "What can I give the world and my fellow travelers?"

I return to love when I understand that love is the greatest life force and the greatest power in the universe.

I return to serenity when I remember that I AM love in its purest form, as I am made of the essence of God.

Positive Change

Sometimes change in our lives is necessary to help us grow, although it may not always be easy. When change occurs, I trust in Divine Spirit to direct my path and my vision.

I give thanks for the past and all the joy, gifts, and lessons it has provided. I reflect on the people I have met and shared experiences with, embracing the role each one has had in the curriculum of my life.

I pause in the present moment and listen to the voice of God, gently, but persistently teaching me how to be a better person. In the quiet of my heart the message comes through that every situation requires integrity and love - always.

I go forward with confidence and enthusiasm, knowing that life is an adventure! I embrace the future, knowing that my needs always have and always will be met. I trust in Divine Providence for prosperity, not only in the form of money and physical needs, but in experiences as well.

When Spirit speaks, allow the positive changes that are necessary for the full experience of life!

Creativity

We all have an innate need to express our individuality. Creativity is that aspect of us that makes us feel alive and unique. It is our soul's expression of itself.

Creativity comes in many forms, such as cooking a meal and presenting it well, decorating a room, creating a flower garden, playing music, and so much more.

When we express our creativity we make the world a more interesting and beautiful place.

When we get caught up in worrying about what other people think, we stifle our creative flow and limit our individuality. Sometimes we are so afraid of rejection that we resist expressing our ideas. Imagine how different the world would be if Thomas Edison, Monet, or the Wright Brothers did not express their creative impulses!

Go ahead, express yourself and create a beautiful day today!

Compassion

Compassion is one of the most beautiful and healing characteristics of not only humanity, but also creation itself. Compassion is demonstrated through the unconditional love and loyalty a beloved pet has for its human family.

Compassion can be seen in the way nature regenerates itself after what is considered natural disasters. I see compassion in nature as Spring begins to bud with new life following Winter, teaching us that new life always follows the difficult periods of our lives.

At times it is easier for us to have compassion for others than it is to have compassion for ourselves. Today I will approach others and myself with a sense of compassion. I will no longer be self destructive in my thoughts, words, or actions. I will strive to see each situation from the other person's perspective. I will stop judging the past and I will be present in the moment.

Accepting Heart

Today I will approach each situation with an open mind and an accepting heart. For it is only in so doing that we are able to experience all that life has to offer.

When Jesus was teaching the Sermon on the Mount he said to the adults, "Let the little children come unto me, for of such is the kingdom of heaven." There is great depth to this statement. When we understand that the kingdom of heaven that he is talking about is complete trust and peace of mind within our hearts, the meaning of his statement becomes clear.

Little children don't spend a lot of time worrying about the state of the world. They do not experience prejudice until taught to do so. They have an uncanny ability to live in the moment and have fun in even the most difficult of situations.

As we go through the experience of life, we begin to take on defense mechanisms and fearful belief systems. These experiences can pull us away from the kingdom of heaven. We can become angry and judgmental and even say it is God's will that we do so. We sometimes create barriers around our heart that keep us from enjoying life.

Let us learn from the children to approach life with enthusiasm and with an accepting heart.

Meditation

Meditation is a practice accepted and recognized by all religious and spiritual practices worldwide. In the practice of meditation, one learns to get in touch with the quiet mind. Where prayer is referred to as speaking to God, meditation is sometimes understood as listening to God or to one's higher Self. For people in deep emotional pain, meditation can be a very difficult process as well as a deeply healing process.

The goal of meditation is to calm our racing thoughts and get in touch with our true and authentic nature. The practice of mindfulness is bringing the scattered mind home and in so doing bringing the different aspects of our being into focus. This is called "peacefully remaining" or "calm abiding."

Calm abiding accomplishes several things. First, all the fragmented aspects of ourselves which have been at war settle, dissolve, and become friends. In that settling, we begin to understand ourselves more, and sometimes even have glimpses of the beauty of our true nature.

People who meditate on a regular basis can effectively change the way their brain responds to situations that would normally move them to an anxious state or into obsessive, looping thoughts. Instead, we learn to enter an alpha state in which the ability to find a solution or state of acceptance becomes easier.

At first, the effects of meditation are temporary, but with consistent meditation, the brain changes over time. Gradually, we gain the ability to enter into the state of calm abiding at will, even when not meditating, and remain there for increasingly longer periods of time.

Meditation is a wonderful practice that, if done consistently, will change your life. But, be patient with yourself. Do not judge your progress. When we have been used to the "monkey chatter," or persistent racing thoughts, meditation can be challenging! Spend five to ten minutes a day focusing only on your breath. When thoughts come in, just let them pass through like a cloud. Let your mind rest.

With a little time and some practice, you will be amazed at the difference in how your mind responds to difficult or challenging situations.

Give yourself the gift of meditation!

Three-Three-Three

Even though I know the peace of God lies within me, there are times when I am drawn away from that understanding. Perhaps I feel challenged by life's circumstances or overwhelmed by my responsibilities. If I wish to return to the peace of God, I needn't go looking for it outside myself. I need only take a moment to remember.

When I am drawn into excess worry or anxiety, I take three seconds to redirect my thinking in a more positive direction. If three seconds isn't enough, I give myself three minutes. I know that if I indulge negative thinking I can turn a small rain cloud into a big typhoon! In that state of mind, it is difficult to make wise decisions and easy to get into self-pity and victim thinking.

When faced with a storm that seems to have no positive outcome, I give myself three hours of quiet time to think and pray. If there are big decisions to be made, I try to give myself three days the think about it. When I give myself time, I make decisions based on wise thought instead of impulsive emotions.

Take a deep breath, and remember three-three-three. When you trust the process, the answers naturally come!

Choose Wisely

Throughout each day, I have the opportunity to make many choices. From the friends I choose to the thoughts I think; everything is a choice, a manifestation of the unlimited possibilities before me.

How I influence people and situations, and how they influence me, is determined by the choices I make. When something doesn't go the way I expect it to, I can choose how I view it and how I respond to it. I can choose to see each situation as a personal affront, or as an opportunity for person growth.

The practice of meditation teaches the lesson of curious observation with non-judgment. This is a powerful tool in allowing the process of life to unfold the gifts it holds for us. This allows me to make choices that are not charged with emotion.

As I prepare for the day, I give thanks for guidance and inspiration in making choices. I call on the inner resources at the core of my being to respond to any situation.

Although in any given moment it might appear that my choices are limited, I know this is an illusion created by my narrow human view. With spiritual eyes, I see infinite possibilities, and I make each choice with confidence and peace.

Choose wisely and create a peaceful day!

Self-Belief

You can achieve anything you put your mind to if you have faith in yourself. However, even when you know you can achieve a goal, it is easy to fall prey to negative thoughts that put you off.

Negative thoughts are typically brought on by our own fear of failure or rejection. If we want to go forward, we need to work through these feelings and let them go. This means that we have to challenge some deeply ingrained beliefs that we may have had since childhood. Maybe we need to get honest about how these beliefs are serving us. It could be that our negative beliefs are an excuse to stay stuck, or maybe they are getting us attention from others, even if it is negative attention.

We have all made mistakes and have done and said things we wish we hadn't. Even if you have made some monumental mistakes in your life, there are some things you have done well! Begin focusing on your positive attributes and work with them.

I began college when I was thirty-five. I had several "failures" behind me that plagued my heart and mind. I was afraid at times, and the work was sometimes daunting, but I finished my PhD when I was fifty. No one had the ability to make me believe that I couldn't do it! Now there are new dreams to achieve.

The past is the past, and serves only as a teacher. Today is a new day, and time for a new beginning. Keep in mind you are a unique individual, with your own talents, gifts, and ideas. There never has, and never will be, another person just like you! With that understanding, you have much to give to the world!

Embrace your goodness! Dare to dream! Always remember, where our thoughts go, energy flows! Whatever you dream, you have the ability to achieve.

Wellness

Wellness is a word we hear a lot these days. But what does it really mean? Basically, it means making good decisions that bring optimal balance to the physical, emotional, mental, and spiritual aspects of one's life.

Physical wellness means that our body is strong and in good condition. Attaining physical wellness encompasses eating nutritious foods that are attractive, enjoyable, and satisfying. Drinking several glasses of water a day helps get rid of the toxins we naturally take in on a daily basis and keeps our vital organs functioning well. Bringing physical balance to our lives includes getting plenty of exercise and fresh air. It is amazing how a few minutes of physical exercise each day can make a big difference in how much energy and stamina we have!

Mental wellness includes feeding our brain with interesting and stimulating information. Many tests have shown that the more we stimulate our thinking, the better our memory is, and the sharper our problem solving skills become. Read a good book, learn a new hobby, and stimulate your brain!

Emotional wellness comes from giving and receiving love. Emotional wellness comes from a having healthy boundaries and good self-esteem. It is important in life to appreciate our uniqueness and live with authenticity. Be happy being you!

Spiritual wellness has to do with our relationship with the vital life-giving source of all that is. I call this source God. Spirituality is different than religion. Religion is the set of guidelines, rituals, and beliefs in which we worship. Spirituality is our relationship with God, others, and ourselves. In order to get in touch with our spiritual dimension is helps to spend time daily in prayer, meditation, and appreciation.

Be well!

Symmetry

Symmetry can be defined as Divine Order. When I trust in Divine Order, outcomes fall into place just as they should.

When I look around, I observe symmetry all around me. I see symmetry in the changing of the seasons, in the cycles of nature, and in the perfect timing that people and situations come into my life.

When things don't make sense, I relax and keep in mind that chaos always comes back to reorganization.

Seeing the Divine Order of the world around me, I am reminded of the symmetry of mind, idea, and expression that allows me to co-create my world in wonderful ways.

I pay attention to the ideas that come to me. When I affirm and build on these ideas I manifest abundance. Each idea, backed by creative action, brings fruit in its season.

Today I will appreciate the symmetry of life. Peacefulness and serenity are my nature, and I will speak words and take actions that promote healing, harmony, goodwill, and joy.

I surrender any need for a specific outcome and celebrate this day and all that it holds!

Responsibility as Personal Power

When things go wrong in our lives, it is our tendency to look around and blame others for our pain and suffering. This is true not only on a personal level, but on a societal and global level as well. Political parties want to blame the other side for the state of our economy and the ills of the world. Religions often base their "rightness" on the "wrongness" of other belief systems to the point of justifying violence and war. Individually, we tend to blame those whom we perceive have wounded us emotionally, mentally, or physically, giving them tremendous power in our lives.

This is not to say that there is not real pain or that there is not true victimization in the world. We all know that there is. But as long as we view ourselves as victims, we cannot heal our hearts, our relationships or our land. When we are in victim mentality we are on the effect end of the principle of cause and effect. This limits our potential for personal growth.

When we honestly look at our lives and begin to take responsibility for our own choices, we gain personal power! When we no longer blame our spouses, ex-spouses, parents, the government, God, or anyone else for our misery, we can take a deep breath and truly be present in the moment. We are then free to have loving and compassionate thoughts for others and ourselves.

When we let go of blame and anger, we can make responsible decisions that bring healing and peace to our lives. Sometimes, this entails making difficult decisions. It may mean that certain relationships in our lives require change, and it may even mean we separate from people, places, and things that are toxic and no longer serve us well.

When we make these decisions in the spirit of peace and loving kindness verses anger and bitterness, we gain personal power. We are no longer victims; we are then on the cause end of the principle of cause and effect.

Let us each effect changes in our world by taking responsibility for our decisions. Let us responsibly bring love and compassion to our environment, to others, and to ourselves.

Fluidity

$\mathcal{S}$ome days it seems like everything just flows and works the way it is supposed to. Other days it seems like there is an obstacle around every corner. This has a great deal to do with mindset.

It is vital to good health to keep our thoughts moving freely, like a swift moving stream. If we let ourselves dwell on mundane concerns or mired down in perceived injustices, our emotions can become blocked and our spirit become disconnected from the Universal energy of life. These blockages can lead to emotional, mental, or physical illness.

When I move from mere belief to the state of KNOWING that God's desire is for me to prosper and live life with abundance, my creative energy begins to flow. My mind becomes clear, and what previously seems like problems to be solved become questions to be answered.

There is plenty in the universe for all of us to prosper. When we get stuck in fear and doubt, we tend to turn to ways of escape or means of perceived security such as alcohol, drugs, or obsessive compulsive behaviors. We begin to view ourselves as victims, as if "they" are out to get us. "They" have as much power as we give them!

When I focus on gratitude, joy, and positive thoughts, good things come my way. I am then able to connect to the vital life-giving energy that turns my dreams into reality!

Loving the Wounded Child

When we have compassion for the wounded child within, instead of condemnation or judgment, change can begin to happen. When we have compassion for ourselves, the God of our understanding becomes a loving co-creator of our lives. A Divine Source that helps us to see our goodness and our character assets. When we see ourselves as God sees us, a perfect creation made in the likeness, image, and essence of him or herself, then what does not serve us well will naturally fall away.

As we learn to understand ourselves better from the perspective of our character assets, we will begin to focus on a life of wellness, health, and loving kindness. When these character traits are what we focus on, they will manifest themselves in our lives. When we fall into what we once viewed as our "character defects," we will feel uncomfortable and out of character.

Addiction is a violent disease that destroys the afflicted person and hurts those who love them. Addiction makes us believe that we are defected human beings that deserve the pain and suffering that the disease brings into our lives. Addictions show up in many ways, including anger, resentments, and self-condemnation.

As we allow the God of our understanding to hold up a mirror in front of us daily, reflecting who we genuinely are, defensive and hurtful behaviors that no longer serve us will fall away.

Epiphany!

An epiphany is a new idea or a deeper understanding of a situation that comes when we do not expect it. An epiphany can make situations that at one moment seemed dark and difficult appear clear and less daunting.

A new idea may present itself at the oddest moment. When we are driving or grocery shopping or taking a walk, a new idea may simply become clear. It is an "aha" moment, a blessing. It may even come in the form of a dream.

Ideas are the activity of God working in and through us, guiding our thoughts and inspiring us to right action. We may not always recognize the ideas that come to us. Sometimes they are fleeting. When we make a conscious effort to open our minds and hearts, epiphanies will naturally appear.

As we move through the day with an expectant attitude and a peaceful heart, let us be an open channel for the wisdom of God.

I look forward to wisdom's expression each day

Expect a miracle today and every day!

Living in The Present Moment

Learning to live in the moment is the easiest way to live. I choose to be at ease with the present moment whatever form it happens to take. This is a moment I do not want to miss.

If I let my mind linger in the past or stray into the future, I might miss the fullness of what life holds for me right now. I am unable to change the past, so I gently let it be and focus on living. I realize I have plans to make for the future--but I do not live there. I live right here in the present moment.

Right now, I have the opportunity to say yes to life, to be alive and aware of the wondrous energy of God coursing through my body.

I live this day one precious moment at a time and enjoy the life I've been given. I am grateful for the fullness of my life and for each golden opportunity to live it well.

I think of the Prayer of Serenity. "God, grant me the serenity to accept the things I cannot change; the courage to change the things I can; and the wisdom to know the difference." This beautiful little prayer teaches us to let go of the past and live in today.

Feeling Centered

There may be times when I wonder if what I want to do serves the highest good. I get caught up in the whirlwind of life where there are deadlines to meet, decisions to make, things to get done, and I begin to feel pulled in many directions. This can make me feel unbalanced.

In those moments, I know that guidance is available to me. I have learned to take time to center myself. I begin by looking within. I know this is where I will find the answers.

I pause and quiet my thoughts. Closing my eyes, I allow my breath to become my focus. My inhale carries wisdom through my heart to every cell of my body. My exhale releases confusion and doubt from my mind. I experience the stillness of the presence of God and gently discern my next step. Doing this only takes a few moments, but it centers me, and I become more confident and peaceful.

When I am centered, I make choices knowing that my desire is to live my life for the highest good of every person and situation that I encounter. I follow the guidance and understanding that I am given.

I understand that I am an expression of love, peace, harmony, and abundance in the world. If my decisions do not line up with this principle, it is a sign that I need to take a few moments and get centered.

Influences

We must decide each day what we will allow to influence our lives. What we put into our mind is what is reflected in our interactions with others. We can choose to be influenced by those who are angry and negative and be part of the problem, or we can choose to see the positive in each situation and be part of the solution.

It is easy to let the world around us inform us of our potential for good. The television, the news, our friends and family all have opinions about the condition of the world and our life potential. The truth is, our potential is limited only by our belief in the limitation!

I work with people with addictions and imbalances in their lives. One person's addiction can bring chaos to the whole family unit, including the grandparents, parents, children, and grandchildren. I also see the miracle of change. When a person does the work to bring their thinking and subsequent behavior back into balance, health can be restored to the whole family. Nothing is impossible!

We are each an integral part of this grand universe, and each one of us can make a positive or negative influence in it! Do you know that the word Uni-verse means one-song? When we bring a loving positive attitude to our individual experiences, collectively we can make positive changes in the world.

Today I choose to let go of the influence of opinions. Whether limited thinking comes from outside of me or from within my own mind, I give it no power or attention. There is a divine creative power within me that is infinite potential. Without limits, I allow God's good to expand in my life.

Released from limiting thoughts, divine ideas fill my life with God's good.

Freedom

Freedom is so important and valuable to us that many are willing to fight and die for it. Freedom is what we believe our country was founded on. Freedom is what gives us the right to choose the type of work that we do, the right to express our thoughts and ideas, and the right to worship as we see fit. This freedom is indeed valuable!

In exercising our freedoms, sometime we imprison ourselves. We become slaves to our excesses, our addictions, and our sense of entitlement. At times our thoughts become roadblocks to our freedom when we are filled with fear, anger, and bitterness.

True freedom comes from within. We are gifted with imagination, which is a God-given ability to see beyond the apparent situation and see a multitude of possibilities.

Whether I am seeking greater financial, emotional, or spiritual abundance, I open myself to Infinite Good -- to God. I break down any barriers I have erected and set a course for success. I trust in the teaching of Jesus, that through faith we may have life, abundantly. That someday we may be truly free.

Now is the Time!

What we believe is what we create in our lives. If I believe in the poverty and destruction of the planet, I will make my decisions according to my belief, therefore manifesting that reality. Instead I choose to see the beauty and constant regeneration that is occurring around me. I can't control other people or situations, but I can control how I relate to them.

At this point in time I am ready to apply my talents and experience life in new ways. I am blossoming, becoming the person I am meant to be. This is my time to stretch, grow, and create the life I want. Regardless of my age or circumstances, divine power and potential are within me. I boldly move forward to accomplish lifelong aspirations.

Perhaps I have dreamt of writing a book, traveling the world, creating a charitable foundation, mastering a new sport, or playing a musical instrument. My destiny is mine to choose and mine to create. Now is the time to take action. With this mindset, my work becomes enjoyable and fulfilling.

Like a flower stretching to the sun, I reach out and open myself to God's good. I choose health, strength, and emotional wellbeing. I trust in my intuition as Divine Inspiration.

How do I know that my intuition in divinely inspired? I check my motive. If my motive is for the good of others and myself, it is Divinely inspired!

Wholeness

Wholeness is the true state of our being. Sometimes it is easy to get so focused on the difficulties in our lives that we do not see or believe beyond that. Whenever we think about letting go of the idea of illness, poverty, or brokenness we begin to say "yeah, but…" This is when we must redirect our thinking.

Life is meant to live abundantly!

Whenever I feel out of alignment with this truth, I stop to calm my thoughts, rest my body, and focus on the healing power of Spirit that moves through me.

Recognizing that I am one with Spirit in mind and body, I embrace this loving life-force flowing through me as the source of my wellbeing. I visualize myself as vital, healthy, well, and whole.

Guided by Spirit, I make wise choices. Nutritious food, energizing exercise, and positive thoughts are staples of my everyday life. I am mindful of balancing work and play, activity, and rest. I set aside time for prayer and quiet contemplation. I live well. I am well.

Truly Free

Why does one driver smile and relax in traffic, while another is tense and irritable? It is a matter of choice. Freedom of choice is an expression of our spiritual freedom, and it affects our attitudes and experiences.

Sometimes it becomes our habit to look for what is wrong in the world, and when we look for what is wrong and what is bad, we find it. When we look for what is good and what is right, we find that too.

When we get caught up looking at the negative in ourselves and in other people, we become irritable, discontent, and even physically and emotionally ill. We all want others to see the best in us and look beyond our flaws. Should we not do the same for our fellow travelers?

Today I have a simple choice: I can be held captive by irritation and restrictive ways of thinking and being, or I can practice genuine spiritual freedom by expressing love in all I think, say, and do.

I choose thoughts and words that are free of disapproval or the need to be right. I choose activities that nurture my body and mind, expressing the freedom of my soul. I choose to treat others in ways that reflect an attitude and spirit of freedom and love.

World Peace

We are all connected in this great web of life, even if we do not recognize it. The great thinkers and writers of antiquity understood this. The idea of interdependence is found in manuscripts and teachings handed down through the centuries.

Mother Teresa was such a person. She believed deeply in the love and respect of all persons. There are two phrases that she said that have had a great impact on my life and on my belief system: "There are many in the world dying for a piece of bread, but there are many more dying for a little love." and "love until it hurts." Mother Teresa was not afraid to walk down war-torn streets or to hold the hand of a dying homeless person. My very favorite quote from Mother Teresa is, "If you invite me to an anti-war rally, I will not come. Invite me to a peace rally, and I will be there." She did not waste her time on causes relating to division. She worked tirelessly for world peace.

Many of us believe this concept on a logical level, but on an emotional and spiritual level we doubt it. We fall into the illusion of division. The illusion of division is created by our ego, and our ego is very often driven by fear, greed, and a lack of consciousness.

Today, look around at how interconnected we all are. Appreciate the differences that make up this beautiful world. Pay attention when you feel fear or judgment. Pray for discernment of how you can bring peace to any situation that brings division.

Love until it hurts.